Why don't they let Poles swim in the ocean?

(page 10)

Why do Jewish girls think prostitution is such good business?

(page 20)

What do you call a black man on a Palomino horse?

(page 22)

Why don't Italians have freckles?

(page 30)

What is a Japanese girl's favorite holiday?

(page 41)

Why don't Arabs get hemorrhoids?

(page 41)

Also by Blanche Knott
Published by Ballantine Books:

TRULY TASTELESS JOKES

TRULY TASTELESS JOKES TWO

Truly Tasteless Jokes Three

* Blanche Knott *

BALLANTINE BOOKS · NEW YORK

 Published in the United States by Ballantine Books, a division of Random House, Inc., New York, and simultaneously in Canada by Random House of Canada Limited, Toronto.

Library of Congress Catalog Card Number: 83-90648

ISBN 0-345-31567-7

Manufactured in the United States of America

First Edition: December 1983

This book is dedicated in true gratitude to the many contributors whose generous spirits and sick minds made it possible.

For TLD—it's all his fault.

Contents

Celebrities

Did you hear about the all-expenses-paid vacation for losers?

—Grace Kelly drives you to the airport.

—Thurman Munson flies you to a remote tropical island.

—Ted Kennedy's your chauffeur on the island.

—You go yachting with Natalie Wood.

—You have drinks with William Holden.

—And Roman Polanski stays home and watches your kids.

*

Why does Nancy Reagan always get on top?

Because Ronnie can only fuck up.

*

What's yellow and sleeps alone?

Yoko Ono.

*

Why can't Santa Claus have babies?

He only comes once a year, and it's down a chimney.

Did you hear Karen Carpenter's brother's new song?
"She Ain't Heavy, She's My Sister."

*

Why is Billie Jean King so good at tennis?
Because she swings both ways.

*

Why does Linda Ronstadt sing so slow?
Because she has a governor on her.

*

What's grosser than grease on Olivia Newton-John?
"Come on Eileen."

*

Have you seen Dolly Parton's new shoes?
Neither has she.

What's the sweat between Dolly Parton's tits?
Mountain Dew.

*

What's Dolly Parton's favorite candy bar?
Mounds.

*

Who is Billie Jean King's latest corporate sponsor?
Snap-On Tools of America.

*

What kind of car does Renée Richards drive?
A convertible.

*

What's fuzzy, smokes, and comes in cubes?
Fidel Castro.

*

What'll it take to reunite the Beatles?
Three more bullets.

*

Did you hear about the Ayatollah Khomeini doll?
Wind it up and it takes Ken and Barbie hostage.

Famous Quotes: "You can never be too rich or too thin."

—Karen Carpenter

*

Clark Gable and the Pope died on the same day. Due to a celestial bureaucratic snafu, the Pope was sent to hell. And Clark Gable went to heaven.

The Pope, obviously in the wrong place, wasn't there five minutes before he had convinced those in charge of the mistake. In the blink of an eye, the Pope was whisked to the pearly gates. As he walked through the portals, he encountered Gable coming out.

"I'm truly sorry about this, my son," said the sympathetic pontiff, "but I've waited my whole life to kneel at the feet of the Blessed Virgin Mary."

Gable flashed his world-famous grin.

"Too late, padre," he said.

*

What is brown, soft, and sits on a piano bench?

Beethoven's First Movement.

Dead Baby

What's small, screams, and can't turn corners?

A baby with a spear through it.

*

What's red and has a million holes in it?

A baby on a bed of nails.

*

What's grosser than 1,000 dead babies stacked one on top of the other?

One live baby on the bottom trying to eat his way out.

*

What's red and silver and crawls into walls?

A baby with forks in its eyes.

*

What's red and white and hangs from a tree?

A baby run over by a snowblower.

*

If you fit ten babies in a test tube using La Machine, and you get them out with a straw, how do you put them back together?

Krazy Glue!

What's red and crawls up your leg?
A homesick abortion.

*

What's more gross than nailing a dead baby to a tree?
Ripping it off!

Helen Keller

How did Helen Keller's parents punish her?
They put extra doorknobs on all the doors.

*

How did they punish her when she wouldn't do her homework?
They stomped on her Braille books with golf shoes.

*

How did they punish her when she *really* misbehaved?
They left the plunger in the toilet.

*

What did Helen Keller say when she fell off the cliff?
Nothing. She had her mittens on.

*

Did you hear about the new Helen Keller disease?
The clap.

Or did you hear about the three panelists on *To Tell the Truth*?

#1: "My name is Helen Keller."
#2: "My name is Helen Keller."
#3: "Mnye nnme ithk Hullne Kwuell."

Polish

A Polish girl was stopped for speeding and hauled down to the police station. The desk sergeant stood up, unzipped his fly, and the girl cried out, "Oh no, not another breathalyzer test!"

*

What's a ski jump?
A Polish whore.

*

What's a Polish cocktail?
A glass of water with a booger in it.

*

Did you hear about the Pole who registered for the draft board at the lumber yard?

*

Two Poles were hunting in the woods when they lost their way. Stanley had read that when lost, you fire three times into the air and help would come. So he did, but nothing happened. An hour later he fired three more times. After another hour his friend Jerzy told him to try a third time.

"Okay," said Stanley, "but we're almost out of arrows."

What's the difference between a Polish girl and a bowling ball?

You can only fit three fingers in a bowling ball.

*

The Polish couple asked their kid what he wanted for his birthday. He said, "I wanna watch." So they let him.

*

Did you hear about the Polish terrorist who tried to blow up a bus?

He burned his lips on the exhaust pipe.

*

Why do Poles make the best astronauts?

Because they take up space in school.

*

Did you hear about the Pole who was found dead in his jail cell with twelve bumps on his head?

He tried to hang himself with a rubber band.

*

Why don't they let Poles swim in the ocean?

Because they leave a ring.

Did you hear about the Pole who thought manual labor was the president of Mexico?

*

What did the Pole do when the doctor found sugar in his urine?

He pissed on his corn flakes.

*

How many Poles does it take to paint a house?

Six thousand and one. One to hold the brush and six thousand to turn the house.

*

Why do Polish people have holes in their faces?

Because when they eat with a fork they always miss their mouths.

*

Did you hear about the new football stadium in Warsaw?

It had to be torn down, because everywhere you sat, you sat behind a Pole.

*

What happens if a Pole doesn't pay his garbage bill?

They stop delivery.

Polish girl: "Daddy, I lost my virginity."
Father: "Did you look under the bed?"

*

Know what a "fuckoff" is?

The tie breaker at a Polish beauty contest.

*

Did you hear about the old Polish man who told his children that his only wish was to be buried at sea?

His two sons drowned digging his grave.

*

An Englishman and a Pole are crossing the Sahara when their camel falls ill. It becomes obvious that the animal desperately needs water, but when they finally reach an oasis, the camel refuses to drink. The two men try every way they can think of to get it to drink, but to no avail. Finally the Pole says, "Listen, I've got an idea. You stick its head in the water and I'll suck on his asshole, and we'll use him as a straw."

A few minutes later the Pole says to the Englishman, "Could you lift his head up a bit? I'm only getting mud from the bottom."

What's Polish shishkebab?
A flaming arrow through a garbage can.

*

What was the Pope's fourth miracle?
He heeled a dog.

*

Why did the Pole flash the Venus de Milo?
He wanted to expose himself to art.

*

Did you hear about the Pole whose husband was out shooting craps?
She didn't know how to cook them.

*

Pole: "Are you Italian?"
Italian: "Why, yes I am."
Pole: "Aloha!"

*

Did you hear about the Pole who went ice fishing?
He came home with a 200-pound chunk of ice.

How did the two Poles get hurt raking leaves?
They fell out of the tree.

*

How do two Poles engage in oral sex?
They stand at opposite ends of the room and yell, "Fuck you!"

*

Why does the new Polish navy have glass-bottomed boats?
So they can see the old Polish navy.

*

How do you sink the Polish navy?
Put it in the water.

*

Twelve Poles were about to rape a German girl, and she screamed, "Nein, nein!"
So three of them left.

*

There are two hippies and a Pole walking down the street. The first hippie's snapping his fingers and saying, "I got rhythm." The second hippie's snapping his fingers and humming, "I got rhythm." They both look over at the Pole, who's busy snapping his fingers too, and ask, "Hey, do you have rhythm?"

"No," says the Pole, "I've got a booger on my finger."

A pro golfer drove into a filling station in his fancy Cadillac. The Polish pump girl noticed some of his golfing equipment on the front seat, and asked the driver about it. So the golfer good-naturedly explained, "Those are tees—I rest my balls on them when I drive."

"Geez," said the Polish girl, "what'll those Cadillac makers think of next?"

*

Did you hear about the Polish girl who thought her period was French Provincial?

*

Who wears a dirty white robe and rides a pig?

Lawrence of Poland.

What's a set of matched Polish luggage?

Two shopping bags from the same store.

*

Remember the Polish woman who thought Moby Dick was a venereal disease?

She also thought asphalt was a proctological condition and that ping-pong balls were a venereal disease from China.

*

How come Poles never make Kool-Aid?

They can never figure out how to get a quart of water into the little envelope.

A 6′8″, 280-pound black man walked into a bar, sat down next to a white guy, and said, "I's big and I's black and I loves to fuck white women!" The guy was so terrified that he put down his beer and ran out of the bar.

The black moved over next to another white man and said, "I's big and I's black and I just loves to fuck white women." The white guy took one look at him, blanched, and ran out of the bar.

The black then went over to a Pole who was having a few at the bar and said, "I's big and I's black and I *loves* to fuck white women."

The Pole looked at him and said, "I don't blame you one bit. I wouldn't fuck a nigger either."

*

Why don't they give a Polish work crew more than half an hour for lunch?

They don't want to have to retrain them.

*

What do they do with old garbage trucks?

Sell them to Poles for campers.

*

How do Polish mothers teach their children to put on their underwear?

Brown in the back, yellow in the front.

What does a Polish businessman carry in his briefcase?

Briefs.

*

A Polish family is sitting around watching TV and the father leans over to the mother and says, "Let's send the kids to the S-H-O-W so we can fuck."

Jewish

What bites but doesn't swallow?
A Jewish girl.

*

Do you know how copper wire was invented?
Two Jews found the same penny.

*

What do you call a JAP on a waterbed?
Lake Placid.

*

How does a JAP call her family for dinner?
"Get in the car, kids!"

*

What's green and hates Jews?
Snotzies.

*

What's a JAP's favorite erotic position?
Bending over the credit cards.

*

What's a Jewish ménage à trois?
Using both hands to masturbate.

How was the Grand Canyon formed?
A Jew dropped a nickel down a gopher hole.

*

This Jewish guy pays a visit to the local whorehouse. He's too cheap to buy a rubber, so instead he wraps the label from his coat around his dick. Needless to say, this falls off *in coitus*, but he never even notices. Later the same day an Irishman purchases the services of the same girl, and just as he's about to come he notices something fall out of her cunt. Picking it up, he reads: "Roth & Stein, Tailors."

"Jesus," he says, "where will those Jews advertise next?"

*

Two Jewish woman are talking. Says Sophie, "Oy, have I got a sore throat."

"When I have a sore throat I suck on a Lifesaver," counsels Sadie.

"Easy for you, you live at the beach."

*

"My daughter lives in a penthouse apartment in Miami," reports Sadie to her friend Sophie. "She goes out to dinner every night at a different restaurant, has beautiful furs and clothes, and lots of boyfriends."

"My daughter's a whore too."

How do Jewish storeowners celebrate Christmas with their families?

They dance around the cash register singing, "What a Friend We Have in Jesus."

*

Why do Jewish girls think prostitution is such good business?

"Ya got it, ya sell it, ya still got it!"

*

What's a JAP's idea of perfect sex?

Simultaneous headaches.

*

First Jew: "Do you like pussy cats?"
Second Jew: "Yes, I do, but Pussy Cohen is okay too!"

*

Two old Jews are standing at the urinals in a men's room. The first Jew glances over and notices that the other one is pissing at an angle.

First Jew: "I see you were circumcised by Rabbi Steinberg."

Second Jew: "I was, but how can you tell?"

First Jew: "He always cuts on a bias."

*

Unaware of each other's presence, an Arab in his tank and an Israeli in his are motoring up opposite sides of the same hill. The two tanks reach the top of the hill at precisely the same instant, and there is a tremendous crash.

The Arab soldier climbs hastily through the hatch of his tank, his arms raised in a gesture of surrender.

Just as quickly, the Israeli leaps from his tank screaming, "WHIPLASH!"

Black

Why do blacks keep chickens in their yards?
To teach their kids how to strut.

*

What do you call a black man on a Palomino horse?
Leroy Rogers.

*

A fisherman from Maine went to Alabama on his vacation. He rented a boat, rowed out to the middle of the lake, and cast his line, but when he looked down into the water he was horrified to see a black man wrapped in chains lying on the bottom of the lake. He quickly rowed to shore and ran to the police station. "Sheriff, sheriff," he gasped, "there's a black guy wrapped in chains, drowned in the lake!"

"Now ain't that just like a nigger," drawled the sheriff, "to take more chain than he can swim with?"

*

What do you call a Mexican Negro?
A wetblack.

*

What do you call holding an orgy at a NAACP meeting?
Getting blackballed.

Did you hear Reagan's staff is creating 500 new jobs for blacks?

They want to expand the National Basketball Association to sixty teams.

Reagan's also appointing a black ambassador ...to the Bermuda Triangle.

*

What do you call 50,000 blacks jumping out of a plane?

Night.

*

Did you hear the NFL is going to use green footballs next year?

Ever hear of a black dropping a watermelon?

*

What do you call two black motorcycle cops?

Chocolate CHiPs.

*

What do you call a black hitchhiker?

Stranded.

*

This second-grade teacher decides that each Friday she'll ask her class a question, a real stumper. If it's answered correctly, everyone gets Monday off.

On the first Friday, she asks, "How many grains of sand are on a beach 50′ × 50′ and 6′ deep?" Needless to say, no one knows the answer.

On the second Friday the teacher asks, "How many gallons of water are there in the Atlantic Ocean?" This one goes unanswered also, and as the weeks go by, the questions don't get any better. Finally one kid gets fed up. On Thursday he paints two marbles black and on Friday he takes them to school, rolling them toward the teacher just as she's about to pose the question. Seeing them, she says, "All right, who's the comedian with the two black balls?

"Bill Cosby!" shouts the kid. "See ya Tuesday."

*

What does the Ku Klux Klan call ten white guys beating on a black man?

A fair fight.

*

What do you call a black woman with braces on her teeth?

A Black and Decker pecker wrecker.

*

A black woman was filling out forms at the welfare office. Under "Number of children," she wrote "10," and where it said "List names of children," she wrote "Leroy." When she handed in the form, the woman behind the desk pointed out, "Now here where it says 'List names of children,' you're supposed to write the names of *each one* of your children."

"Dey all named Leroy," said the black woman.

"That's very unusual. When you call them, how

do they know which one you want?" asked the welfare worker.

"Oh, den I uses de last names."

*

What's big and white and lives on the bottom of the ocean?

Ku Klux Clam.

*

The NAACP sent an agent to Alabama to check the progress in integration of churches. After a few weeks of checking around, he called headquarters to file his report. "How about the Catholics?" asks his boss.

"The Catholics are doing okay; they got the right idea."

"What about the Methodists?"

"They've come a long way," says the agent. "They're doing just fine."

"And the Baptists?" asks the boss.

"I just want to know one thing—when they baptize you, how long are they supposed to hold you under?"

This big black guy is in the Cadillac showroom eyeballing the most deluxe model, and over his face comes a grin that just won't quit. Perplexed, the car salesman comes up to him and asks, "Excuse me, sir, but are you thinking of buying that car?"

"I ain't thinking about buying that car," came the answer. "I is *gonna* buy that car."

"Very good, sir. But that car's very expensive—why are you smiling so much?"

"Cause I'm thinkin' about pussy!"

*

There's a new video game called Black Man:

It has two big lips that chase watermelons around the screen.

*

What do you call a black Smurf?

A Smigger.

*

A black guy riding down the road in his new Caddie is so busy waving to his admirers that he completely misses the turn. Over the five-hundred-foot cliff plunges the car, to be smashed into pieces at the bottom—but no black man in sight. Finally we see him, fifty feet from the top of the cliff, clinging to a stunted bush with all his strength. "Dear Lord," he prays, "I never asked you for nothin' before, but I'm asking you now: Save me, Lord, save me."

Booms the Lord: "LET GO OF THE BRANCH."

"But Lord, if I do that I'll fall."

"TRUST ME. LET GO OF THE BRANCH."

"But Lord, I'm gonna fall and die. . . ."

"TRUST ME. HAVE I EVER LIED TO YOU BEFORE? LET GO OF THE BRANCH."

"No, Lord, you've never lied to me. Okay, here I go." And he falls to his death.

"DUMB NIGGER."

*

What kind of candy should you send a black virgin on Valentine's Day?

Chocolate-covered cherries.

*

Why does Georgia have blacks and California have earthquakes?

California had first pick.

*

What do you get when you cross a black with Bo Derek?

A "Ten of Spades."

Why don't blacks drive convertibles?

Because their lips would flap them to death.

*

What happens when you put an Odor-Eater in a black man's shoes?

He disappears.

*

What is sickle-cell anemia?

AIDS for spades.

*

What does this mean: $\frac{1SS}{1SB} - R = 3NOW$

One soul sister on top of a soul brother, minus a rubber, equals three niggers on welfare.

*

There was once a wealthy Texan who had an unreasonable dislike for elephants. Realizing that it was a problem, he consulted a psychiatrist. The shrink told him, "This is a fairly common ailment and the cure is simple: You must go to Africa and shoot an elephant." That sounded like a good idea, so the Texan flew to Africa and hired a Great White Hunter to take him on a safari to shoot an elephant. Working for the hunter was a local native who, in turn, hired a bunch of his fellows to spread out in a long line, blow horns, beat drums, and drive the elephants toward the elephant-blind where the hunters were waiting. As they waited for the elephant to come, there was suddenly lots of thrashing and bellowing in the bushes, and out came the Head Beater. The Texan shot him right between the eyes. The Great White Hunter became very irate. "What the hell did you do that for? He's a good friend of mine; we've been together for twenty years!"

The Texan replied, "If there's anything I hate worse than elephants, it's big black noisy niggers!"

*

What does a little black kid say as he's walking back and forth alongside a zebra?

"Now you see me, now you don't. Now you see me, now you don't."

Italian

What's red, green, blue, yellow, purple, and orange?

An Italian dressed up.

*

What's the definition of a cad?

An Italian who doesn't tell his wife he's sterile until after she's pregnant.

*

Have you heard about the Italian girl who flunked her driver's license test?

When the car stalled, from force of habit she jumped into the back seat.

*

Did you hear about the Italian who was asked to be a Jehovah's Witness?

He refused because he didn't see the accident.

*

What do you call an Italian who marries a black?

A social climber.

*

Why don't Italians have freckles?

Because they slide off.

Why do Italians wear hats?
So they know which end to wipe.

*

What do you call an Italian with an IQ of 180?
Sicily.

*

A little Italian kid was helping the construction crew build a house next door to his. He was acting just like the crewmen, swinging his little plastic tools around and swearing up a storm just like them. His mother wasn't too pleased when she came to get him for lunch and overheard the kid saying loudly, "Fuckin' shit, pass me another goddamn nail." His mother grabbed him by the hand, pulled him inside the house, and said, "Giuseppe, I'm warning you—if your papa ever hears you talking like that, you're gonna be plenty sorry."

Hearing of Giuseppe's misbehavior on his return home from work, the father said, "Son, I've got to teach you a lesson. Go out in the back and get me a switch."

"Fuck you," said Giuseppe, "that's the electrician's job!"

*

Did you hear about the Italian who:
—Spent four days in Sears looking for wheels for a miscarriage?
—Took his expectant wife to the grocery store because they had free delivery?
—Took a roll of toilet paper to a crap game?

—Lost his girlfriend because he couldn't remember where he laid her?
—Wouldn't go out with his wife because she was a married woman?
—Bought his wife a washer and dryer for Christmas—a douche bag and a towel?
—Moved his house two feet back to tighten the clothesline?

*

How can you tell Italian women are embarrassed by their long black hair?

Because they wear long black gloves to cover it up.

*

How does an Italian count his goats?

He counts the legs and divides by four.

*

How can you tell an Italian with kidney trouble?

He's the one with the rusty zipper and yellow tennis shoes.

*

Why are garbage cans painted international orange?

So little Italian children will think they're eating at Howard Johnson's.

Did you hear about the Italian who cleaned out his ears and his head caved in?

Ethnic Jokes - Variegated

Who are the four most dangerous people in the world?

A Jew with money, a Greek with tennis shoes, a Puerto Rican with a knife, and a Polack with brains.

*

What do you get when you cross a Jew with a gypsy?

A chain of empty stores.

*

A French couple, an Irish couple, and a Polish couple are having dinner together. The Frenchman says to his wife, "Pass me the sugar, sugar."

Not to be outdone, the Irishman says, "Could you pass me the honey, honey?"

Most impressed by these clever endearments, the Pole leans over to his wife and says, "Pass me the pork, pig."

Know what these are?

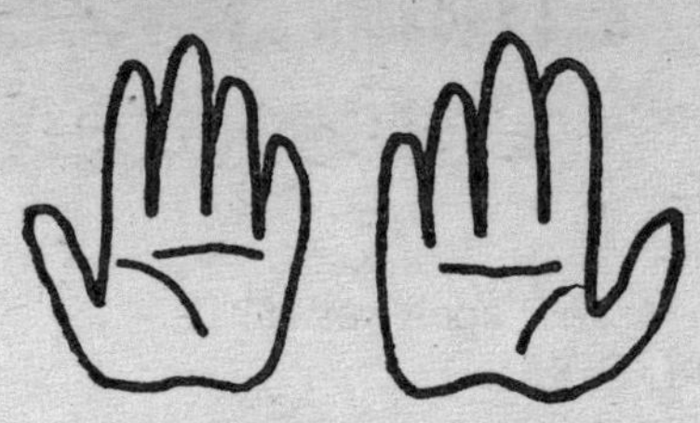

Polish silverware

Italian vibrator

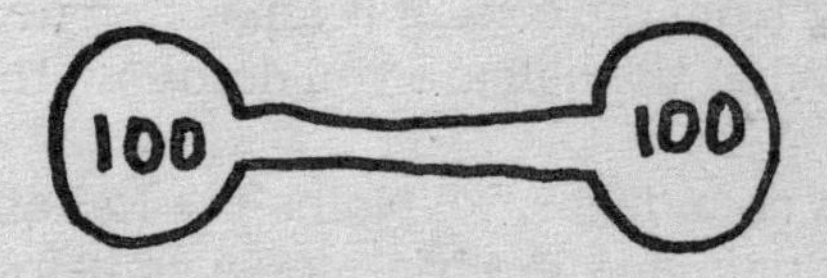

Jewish suppository

*

A Pole, an Italian, and a Jew, all first-time fathers, are pacing nervously in the maternity ward waiting room when a nurse rushes out of the delivery room holding a black baby. "Is it yours?" she asks the Italian.

"Certainly not," he retorts.

"Yours?" she asks the Pole, who vigorously denies paternity.

"How about you?" she asks the Jew.

"Maybe," he says glumly. "My wife burns everything."

How does a JAP spell relief?

R-O-L-E-X.

*

How does a Pole spell relief?

F-A-R-T.

*

During a routine check of a construction site, the foreman finds an Italian construction worker hanging from the ceiling beams of an unfinished room. "What the hell are you doing up there?" he asks.

"I'm a chandelier," explains the Italian.

"Get down and get back to work before I bust your head," growls the foreman, but to no avail, for on several subsequent checks he finds the Italian in exactly the same position. Finally he has to fire him. The next morning he is infuriated to catch all the Polish workers on the site packing up and getting ready to leave. "What the *hell* do you clowns think you're doing?" he shouts.

"Hey listen," say the Poles, "we ain't working without no lights."

*

What's transparent and lies in the gutter?

A Pakistani with the shit kicked out of him.

Why aren't there any swimming pools in Mexico?
Because all the Mexicans who can swim are over here.

*

Why did the Mexicans fight so hard to take the Alamo?
So they could have four clean walls to write on.

*

Definition of a Mexican wolf:
Hot tamale looking for a frijole.

*

Why do Mexicans eat beans every day?
So they can take a bubble bath at night.

*

Have you heard about the new Mexican war movie?
It's called A Tacolips Now.

*

Why do Indians wear jock straps?
Totem pole.

*

What do you call an Oriental person on Quaaludes?
A mello-yellow.

What's the Chinese word for watermelon?
Coon-chow.

*

How many sand-niggers (Arabs) does it take to change a light bulb?
Three: One to hold the bulb and two to turn the stool. But they need a foreign advisor to tell them it was burned out.

*

In Greece, how do they separate the men from the boys?
With a crowbar.

*

What's the Greek army's motto?
"Never Leave Your Buddy's Behind."

*

How do you distinguish the clans in Scotland?
If there's a quarter-pounder under his kilt, he's a MacDonald.

*

What's the difference between an Irish wedding and an Irish wake?
One less drunken Irishman.

*

What do Arabs do on a Saturday night?
Sit under palm trees and eat their dates.

What positions do WASPS fuck in?
"POSITIONS?!?"

*

An Arab diplomat visiting the U.S. for the first time was being wined and dined by the State Department. The Grand Emir was unused to the salt in American foods (french fries, cheeses, anchovies, etc.), and was constantly sending his manservant Abdul to fetch him a glass of water. Time and time again Abdul would scamper off and return with a glass of water, but then came the time when he returned empty-handed.

"Abdul, you bastard son of an ugly camel, where is my water?" demanded the Grand Emir.

"A thousand pardons, O Illustrious One," stammered the wretched Abdul. "White man sit on well."

*

Did you know that 85% of all Japanese men have Cataracts?

The rest drive Rincolns and Chevlorets.

*

The sheriff arrived at the scene of the horrible accident just as his deputy, all alone, was climbing down from the controls of a bulldozer. "Say, Junior, what's goin' on?" asked the sheriff.

"A bus full of migrant workers went out of control and over the cliff, and I just finished burying 'em," explained the deputy.

"Good work, boy," said the sheriff. "Pretty gory work—were all of 'em dead?"

Junior nodded sadly and said, "Some of 'em *said* they weren't, but you know how them Mexicans lie."

*

What's gross ignorance?

One hundred and forty-four Irishmen.

*

When a Polish immigrant moved to a small town in Georgia, he asked one of the locals what they did for amusement.

"Why, we go down to the bowlin' alley and beat up Negroes," came the casual reply.

That night, the Pole followed his new friend to the bowling alley. Sure enough, a group of blacks came in, and the Georgia boys started beating them up.

Anxious to please his new friends, the Pole took a club and commenced smashing bowling balls.

"What in hell are you doin'?" asked one of the startled Georgians.

"You get the adults," replied the agitated Pole, "and I'll take care of the eggs!"

*

An Italian, an American, and a Pole were to be executed by a firing squad. The Italian was called up first.... "Ready... Aim..." The Italian, thinking quickly, shouted, "TORNADO!!!" Every man ran for cover and the Italian escaped. The American went up next.... "Ready... Aim..." "HURRICANE!!!" he shouted, and the American escaped.

The Pole went next. He was wondering what to say. "Ready . . . Aim . . . FIRE!"

*

What is a Japanese girl's favorite holiday?
Erection day!

*

Two Englishmen in darkest Africa got hungry and dropped into a native restaurant in a small village. They received menus and noticed a fair variety of dishes. Broiled Spaniard was $3.50, including salad and dessert. Fried Frenchman, with a side order of vegetables, cost $3.75. Stewed Swiss ran $3.25. But Baked Arab was listed at $10.50.

They called the waiter. "Why?" asked one. "Are the Arabs that delicious?"

"No," replied the waiter. "They all taste about the same."

"But the price is so high," the Englishman protested. "There must be some reason."

"Oh," the waiter said. "There is a good reason. Did you ever try to clean an Arab?"

*

Why don't Arabs get hemorrhoids?
Because they are such perfect assholes.

*

It's a busy evening in a bar on the outskirts of Las Vegas. A drunken Indian comes in packing a shotgun, holding a dead cat by the tail in one hand, and a five-gallon bucket filled with cow manure in the other. Without warning, he shoots one round of bullets into the bucket and chews a huge hole in the cat. At the sight of this, customers start to leave, and the bartender asks the Indian to go to a more secluded part of the bar.

The Indian does so reluctantly, but still continues his acts, grossing out the customers. The bartender finally goes over and asks the Indian, "Will you please leave now? I'm losing business because of you. Why are you doing this?" The Indian looks surprised for a second and replies, "Me wanna be like white man. Me wanna go get drunk, shoot the shit, and eat pussy."

*

An Irishman, an Italian, and a Pole in Mexico got drunk and killed a Mexican. All three went to jail and were sentenced to the electric chair. First, they sat the Irishman down and asked him if he had any last words. He said he was a dentist and would care for everyone in the village for twenty-five years if they would let him go. They said they were sorry, but they had to carry out the electrocution. They pulled the switch and nothing happened.

The executioner said that by law, the Irishman was free to go because the electric chair hadn't worked. Then the Italian sat down. The same question was asked. He said he was a medical school graduate and would care for the villagers for twenty-five years in exchange for his freedom. Again, the answer was no. The switch was pulled and nothing happened. He too was set free.

Then the Pole sat down. When asked if he had any last words, the Pole said that he was a graduate in electrical engineering and, he told the executioner, "If you'll put that little white wire in that hole, and the little red wire in that hole..."

*

At a doctors' convention in Switzerland, a conversation was taking place in a tavern after the day's lectures were over. An Israeli doctor said, "Medicine in my country is so advanced that we can take a kidney out of one person and put it in another and have him looking for work in six weeks."

A German doctor said, "That's nothing. In Germany, we can take a lung out of one person and put it in someone else and have him looking for work in four weeks."

A Russian doctor said, "In my country, medicine is so advanced that we can take half a heart from one person, put it in another, and have them both looking for work in two weeks."

An American doctor, not wanting to be outdone, said, "That's nothing. We can take an *asshole* out of *Hollywood*, put him in the *White House*, and have half the nation looking for work the next day."

Handicapped

A man went into a bar after work one day, and after a beer or two he noticed a man passed out in the corner. After an hour or so the fellow was still very drunk and incoherent, so, being a nice guy, the first man decided to take him home. He looked up the drunk's address in his wallet, then started struggling to get the man out to his car. Dragging, heaving, and finally carrying the man, he finally reached his car; then the process had to be repeated in front of the drunk's house. At last the nice guy got the man up to the door and rang the bell, which was promptly answered by a pleasant-looking woman.

"Oh, thank you so much for bringing him home," she said. "But where's his wheelchair?"

*

A man with a very bad lisp went into a store to buy some nuts. "How muth are your cathews?" he asked the fellow behind the counter.

"Fifteen dollars a pound," answered the storekeeper.

"How muth are your pecanth?"

"Twenty dollars a pound," was the answer.

"And the peanuths?" he lisped.

"Eight dollars a pound."

"Okay," said the customer, "I'll take half a pound of pecanth and half a pound of peanuth, and thankth for not making fun of my lithp."

"I understand," said the storekeeper kindly. "You see, I have a rather big nose."

"Goth, ith that your noth? I thought your nuth were tho high that that wath your dick!"

*

A guy is standing at a urinal when he notices that he's being watched by a midget. Although the little fellow is staring at him intently, the guy doesn't get uncomfortable until the midget drags a small stepladder up next to him, climbs it, and proceeds to admire his privates at close range. "Wow," comments the midget, "those are the nicest balls I have ever seen!"

Surprised—and flattered—the man thanks the midget and starts to move away.

"Listen, I know this is a rather strange request," says the little fellow, "but I wonder if you would mind if I touched them." Again the man is rather startled, but seeing no real harm in it, he obliges the request.

The midget reaches out, gets a tight grip on the man's balls, and says loudly, "Okay, hand over your wallet or I'll jump!"

*

What do you call a hooker with no legs?

A nightcrawler.

*

What do you call a girl who's just been run over by a car?

Patty.

What do you call a man who has a toe growing here (point to knee)?

Tony.

*

What do you call a guy with no arms or legs, on the bottom of the ocean?

Sandy.

*

What do you call the same guy in a pile of leaves?

Russell.

*

One day in the bell tower, Quasimodo decides he wants a day off at least once a week. He puts an ad in the paper and an armless dwarf applies for the job. Quasimodo asks him how he can possibly ring the bell and the armless dwarf says, "Watch this!" He takes a running start and hits the bell with his face to ring it. Then he takes another running start and rings the bell again. Then he takes another running start and misses the bell and falls out the window of the tower. When the police come to ask for witnesses they ask Quasimodo if he knows the man's name. Quasimodo replies, "No, but his face rings a bell."

*

Little Johnny was showing off his homemade motor scooter to his best friend, Jimmy.

"Where'd you get the motor?" asked Jimmy.

"My dad's iron lung," said Johnny.

"What did your dad say about that?" asked Jimmy.

"'AARRGGHHH!'" said Johnny.

Even More Jokes for the Blind

Male Anatomy

A guy finds a lamp lying on the beach, and, being the ever-hopeful type, he rubs it. Sure enough, after a few minutes a genie appears and offers to grant him his greatest wish. Without a second's hesitation the guy says, "I want a dick that can touch the ground."

So the genie cuts his legs off.

*

Why did the rubber fly across the room?

It got pissed off.

*

What's the only thing the government can't tax?

A penis, because 90% of the time it's inactive, 10% of the time it's in the hole, and it's got two dependents and they're both nuts.

*

What's the ultimate rejection?

When you're masturbating and your hand falls asleep.

*

What's the definition of skyjacking?

A handjob at 32,000 feet.

A young man was spending the night at the apartment of a married couple of his acquaintance. Since they had no couch, the couple decided to share their bed with the guest, and they all retired early.

It wasn't long afterwards that the wife whispered in the young man's ear, "Pull a hair from my husband's butt; if he's asleep we can make love."

The young man did as instructed, and after getting no response from the husband, he proceeded to make it with the wife. Not feeling completely satisfied, the wife proceeded to propose the same course of action a second time, and later a third time, and the young man was only too happy to oblige.

Finally the husband rolled over and said wearily, "Listen, it's bad enough that you're fucking my wife in the same bed as me, but do you have to use my ass as a scoreboard?"

*

A man was at the urinal in a public restroom when a big black man rushed in, whipped out a twelve-incher, and said, "Whew, I just made it."

The first guy looked over and said, "Can you make me one too?"

*

What's this? (Make a fist and kiss each of the knuckles.)

Foreplay before masturbation.

Why is a dick like Rubik's Cube?

The more you play with it, the harder it gets.

*

An inquisitive young man was on a flight to Hawaii and was having a few drinks to celebrate his upcoming vacation, so he was quite alarmed to discover that the men's room was under repair. So he asked the stewardess for admittance to the ladies' room. "Certainly," said the stewardess, "as long as you don't touch the WW button, the PP button, or the ATR button." Of course the young man agreed.

But no sooner had he relieved himself than his curiosity got the better of him. He pressed the WW button and soon enjoyed the sensation of warm water being sprayed up onto his rear end. This first experiment was so pleasant that he had no hesitation in reaching for the PP button, and was rewarded by the soft pat of a powder puff on his bottom. Much emboldened by his first two trys, he pressed the ATR button.

The next thing he knew he was waking up in a bright, white room with a nurse standing by his bedside. "What happened?" he asked groggily.

"You pushed the WW button, right?" said the nurse, with a knowing look in her eye.

"Yes," the young man admitted.

"You also pushed the PP button, right?"

"Yes."

"And then you pushed the ATR button, am I correct?"

"Yeah, so?"

"ATR stands for Automatic Tampon Removal. By the way, your penis is on your pillow."

Definition of a jock strap:
An All-American ball carrier.

*

What do a cobra and a two-inch cock have in common?
No one wants to fuck with either of them.

*

Why shouldn't you suck a twelve-inch cock?
You could get foot-in-mouth disease.

*

A week before his wedding a young farmer fell off his barn roof into a pile of manure. A bit shaken, he went to the doctor for a checkup. After looking him over, the doctor said, "Well, Tom, you were really pretty lucky, but I do have a bit of bad news for you. When you fell you broke your penis. I can put a splint on it though, and you should be good as new in about two weeks." Of course this didn't make Tom very happy, but since there was nothing he could do about it, he decided to wait until the wedding night to tell his bride and hope she wouldn't be too upset.

Following the festivities the next week, Tom and his new bride checked into the honeymoon suite at the local motel. Tom still had not mentioned anything about the unfortunate accident. Soon his bride came out of the bathroom wearing a very skimpy nightie, blushed, and said, "Tom, darling, as you know I have never been with a man before. . . ."

Realizing it was now or never, Tom summoned

up all his courage, pulled down his shorts, and said, "Louise, I have never been with a woman either. See, mine is still in the crate."

*

What's worse than a fellatrix with overbite?

A cunnilinguist with five o'clock shadow.

*

What's the difference between light and hard?

1) It's light all day.
2) You can sleep with a light on.

*

What's the difference between a snowman and a snowwoman?

Snowballs.

*

Old Pa Jones tells Old Ma Jones that he's going into town today to apply for Social Security. Ma says, "But Pa, you don't have a birth certificate. How are you gonna prove your age?"

"Now don't you worry, Ma," say Pa, and leaves for town. Sure enough he's back in a few hours and reports that he'll be getting the first check in just three weeks.

"So how'd ya prove your age?" asks Ma.

"Easy," says Pa, smiling. "I just unbuttoned by shirt and showed 'em all the gray hairs on my chest."

"Well, while you were at it," scolds Ma, "why didn't you drop your pants and apply for disability?"

What do you do in case of fallout?

Put it back in and take shorter strokes.

*

One spring day two men were out in the woods hunting. Feeling a sudden need to relieve himself, George went over to a nearby clump of bushes, unzipped his fly, and started in when a poisonous snake lunged out of the greenery and bit him on his prick. Hearing George's howl of pain and fright, his friend Fred came running up and told him to lie still while he rushed into town for a doctor.

"There's only one way to save your friend's life," said the doctor gravely. "If you cut an 'X' over the bite and then suck all the poison out, he'll probably be okay, but otherwise there's not much hope."

Hearing Fred's footsteps, George rose weakly up on one elbow and cried out, "Fred, what'd he say? What did the doctor say?"

"George, old friend," said Fred sadly, "he said you're gonna die."

*

What do you get when you cross a stud with a debtor?

Someone always into you for at least ten inches.

*

An eighty-year-old man drops by the local sperm bank and offers to make a donation. The pleasant orderly tries politely to explain how the sperm bank works, suggesting that perhaps he isn't up to making a deposit. But there's no dissuading the old codger, and finally they give up and show him to a cubicle. After two hours the old man has not emerged, so a nurse is sent in to check on him.

Seeing her, the old man exclaims petulantly, "I tried it with my right hand. Then I tried it with my left hand. I even hit it up against the toilet a few times, but I still can't get the top off this little bottle!"

*

What can Lifesavers do that a man can't?
Come in five different flavors.

*

Grafitti: "I'm 10″ long and 3″ wide. Interested?"
"Fascinated. How big is your dick?"

*

A guy wandered into the women's rest room and casually unzipped his fly.

"Sir," said a woman sternly. "this is for *ladies*!"

"Yeah?" he said. "So's this!"

*

This man had such bad luck that when he picked up his shirt out of the drawer, all the buttons fell off. Then when he picked up his attaché case, the handle fell off. And for three days, he was afraid to go to the bathroom.

After a pleasant date the guy parked his car two hundred yards from the girl's apartment, pulled out his cock, and placed her left hand on it. She slapped him with her right hand, got out of the car, walked the two hundred yards home, turned around, and screamed, "I got two words for you: *Drop dead*!"

"And I got two words for you," he screamed back. "LET GO!"

*

What's the definition of macho?

Jogging home from your own vasectomy.

*

At her annual checkup, the attractive young woman is told by the doctor that it's necessary to take her temperature rectally. She agrees, but a few minutes later says indignantly, "Doctor, that's not my rectum!"

"Madam," says the doctor, "that's not my thermometer."

Just then the woman's husband, who's come to pick her up, comes into the room. "Just what the hell is going on here?" he demands.

"I'm taking your wife's temperature," the doctor coolly explains.

"Okay, doctor," says the husband, "but that thing better have numbers on it."

*

There was a woman who couldn't get enough, so she put an ad in the paper. The very next afternoon a man came to her front door, and she asked to see his dick. "I'm sorry, young man," she explained, "but it must be ten feet long. Come back in a week."

A week passed and the doorbell rang again. "Well," said the woman, "it's two feet long. Come back in a week and we'll see what we can do."

Another week went by and the man had to ring the doorbell with his dick wrapped around his neck. "Not bad," said the woman, "but you've still got a foot to go."

"Wait a minute," said the man. "I brought this crank with me." He finally stretched it out to a full ten feet, and the woman said, "All right, let's go to the bedroom."

The woman undressed and the man got a hard-on and strangled himself.

*

Three old men were sitting around talking about who had the worst health problems. The seventy-year-old said, "Have I got a problem. Every morning I get up at 7:30 and have to take a piss, but I have to stand at the toilet for an hour 'cause my pee barely trickles out."

"Heck, that's nothing," said the eighty-year-old. "Every morning at 8:30 I have to take a shit, but I have to sit on the can for hours because of my constipation. It's terrible."

The ninety-year-old said, "You guys think *you* have problems! Every morning at 7:30 I piss like a racehorse, and at 8:30 I shit like a pig. The trouble with me is, I don't wake up till eleven."

A young playboy steps into a bar looking for some action. He's delighted to see a gorgeous blonde walk in, but she goes right past him, heads for a table in the back, and cosies up to an old, dirty derelict nursing a whisky. Five minutes later a lovely brunette comes into the bar, but she too makes a beeline for the back table and sits on the other side of the old alcoholic.

Quite at a loss, the young stud leans over and asks the bartender if he knows what's going on.

"I dunno," says the bartender. "He comes in every day, orders a whisky, sits in the back, and licks his eyebrows."

*

Why did God create men?

Because you can't teach an electric vibrator to mow the lawn.

*

A woman was throwing a costume party where everyone had to dress up as an emotion in order to be admitted. She was at the door when the first guest arrived, dressed in blue. "Aha," she said. "I see you must be the blues." The guest nodded and went inside. The next guest was in green, and she said, "I bet you're green with envy." The guest nodded and went inside. The next guest showed up completely naked but had a bowl of custard strapped around his waist and his penis was stuck in the middle of it. The hostess couldn't figure out what he was, so she inquired. The guest replied, "I'm fucking disgusted."

What's this? (Open your mouth wide and stick out your tongue.)

Blow-jobber's cramp.

*

A man at a nudist camp got a letter from his mom asking him for his picture. Since the only pictures he had were taken in the nude, he cut one in half and mailed her one from the waist up.

His mom wrote back after receiving the photo and said, "Can your grandma have one too?" The man thought, Since Grandma can't see well, I'll give her the bottom half. So he sent it.

After getting her grandson's picture, she wrote to him and said, "Nice picture, but your hairstyle makes your nose look long."

*

A woman went into the neighborhood grocery store and asked the grocer for a can of cat food. The grocer knew the woman and knew that she didn't have a cat. So he asked why she was buying the cat food. The woman replied, "It's for my husband's lunch." The grocer was shocked and said, "You can't feed cat food to your husband! It will kill him."

"I've been giving it to him for a week now, and he really likes it!" she replied.

And so each day, the woman would come in and buy a can of cat food for her husband's lunch. One day the grocer happened to be scanning the obituary column of the local paper and noticed that the woman's husband had passed away. When she came into the store a few days later, he said to her, "I'm sorry to hear about your husband, but

I told you that if you kept on giving him cat food it would kill him."

The woman replied, "It wasn't the cat food that killed him. He broke his neck trying to lick his ass!"

*

Then there was a woman who was divorcing her husband on the grounds of "hobosexuality." "Don't you mean *homo*sexuality," her friend asked. "No, hobosexuality. He's a bum fuck."

A guy got a sunburn at a nude beach. Later, he found lovemaking unbearable, so he went to the kitchen, poured a tall glass of milk, and inserted himself. His girlfriend, watching from the door, said, "I've always wanted to know how men reloaded that thing!"

*

A new lumberjack had just finished his first month in the lonely wilds of Alaska, where there were no women for miles. He finally couldn't take it anymore and nervously asked the foreman what the men did to relieve the pressure.

"Try the hole in the barrel outside the shower," suggested the foreman. "The men swear by it."

The lumberjack dubiously tried it out and had the experience of his life. "That barrel is fantastic!" he said. "I'm going to use it every day!"

"Every day but Wednesday," the foreman said.

"Why not Wednesday?"

"That's your day in the barrel."

A man is very horny, but also very broke. He manages to scrape up two dollars, however, and goes to the local whorehouse. The madam looks at his money and laughs. She explains that for two dollars there's a special cheapskate room. She ushers him down the hall and shows him into a room, leaving and closing the door behind her. In the room is a full-length mirror and a duck. The man looks at this, and says to himself, I'm not going to fuck a duck. However, after thinking it over, he remembers how horny he is, and figures, What the hell, I'll try anything once. A week later, he's horny again, but even more broke. He goes to the whorehouse with his last dollar. The madam laughs and tells him that for one dollar he can't fuck anything, but he can see a good show. She ushers him into a room where several men are gathered around a one-way window, laughing and screeching. Approaching the window, the man sees a guy getting it on with a goat. Remembering last week, he uncomfortably says, "I don't see what's so funny." One of the spectators turns to him and says, "It's not as funny as last week. We had a guy here who was doing it with a duck!"

*

What are the five worst things about being a penis?

—You have a hole in your head.

—You have permanent ring-around-the-collar.

—Your next-door neighbors are two nuts and an asshole.

—Your best friend is a cunt.

—Every time you get excited, you throw up.

Female Anatomy

Why did God give women nipples?
To make suckers out of men.

*

Why did the Detroit Lions hire two nuns and a prostitute for the new season?
Because they needed two tight ends and a wide receiver.

*

A fellow goes to confession and tells the priest, "Father, I've had an affair with another woman."

"I see," says the priest, looking grave. "But I cannot grant you absolution until you tell me who she is."

"Well, okay, Father," says the guy somewhat reluctantly. "Her name is Pussy Green, and she's a blonde and a knockout."

The following Sunday this gorgeous blonde makes her way down the aisle and into the front pew. The priest takes a few good looks and finally asks the altar boy, "Son, is that Pussy Green?"

The altar boy stoops down and peers, then says, "No, Father, I think that's just the reflection from the stained glass windows."

*

Why are clams like women?
When the red tide comes, you don't eat them.

Three old ladies were sitting on a park bench when a flasher walked up to them and displayed his endowments. The first old lady had a stroke, the second old lady had a stroke, but the third old lady's arms were too short to reach.

*

Part of a certain Avon lady's territory included a ten-story high-rise apartment complex, and she had a favorite customer on the eighth floor. While on her way out of the elevator to pay a sales call, the Avon lady realized she was about to pass some gas. Looking around and not finding anyplace more appropriate, she quickly darted back into the empty elevator and relieved herself. The aroma was particularly lethal, so she rummaged through her Avon bag until she came across some pine-scented spray, with which she liberally doused the elevator.

By this time the elevator was back to the ground floor, and when the doors opened a drunk reeled in. The Avon lady tried to look nonchalant, pushing the button for the eighth floor, but the drunk kept sniffing around and eyeing her suspiciously. Finally she asked stiffly, "Is something wrong, sir?"

"Well I don't know about you, lady," said the drunk, "but it smells like someone took a shit on a Christmas tree in here!"

*

How does a man know when he's eaten pussy well?

When he wakes up in the morning and his face looks like a glazed doughnut.

Three young women were hired by an insurance company on the same day. A year later the boss said each of them was due for a promotion, and that each woman would get her own office with her name on the door.

One day one of the women came in and found to her surprise and dismay that the other two had already moved into their own offices. Going into her boss's office, she asked when her own office would be provided.

He pulled back his chair from his desk and unzipped his fly. "See this?" he asked. "This is quality. And in this company, quality goes in before the name goes on."

*

Did you hear about the new video game for women only, called Dick-Man?

You put in a quarter and get fucked.

*

Two old ladies are sitting on their rocking chairs out in front of the nursing home when Lucy turns to her friend and asks, "Mildred, do you remember the minuet?"

"Good heavens, no," replies Mildred. "I don't even remember the ones I fucked."

*

I've got a joke so funny it'll make your breasts fall off:

Oh . . . I see you've already heard it.

Bert and Ethel were debating whether they should get a house pet, and if so, what kind. At long last Bert decided a bear would be just the thing, but Ethel was skeptical. "Honey," she said, "where will the bear eat?"

"No problem," said Bert. "We'll train him to eat at the table with us."

"But where will it go to the bathroom?"

"Don't worry, Ethel, we'll train it to use the toilet just like we do."

"Well, where will the bear sleep?"

"He can sleep with us," was Bert's answer.

"Sleep with *us*!" shrieked Ethel. "What about the smell?"

"Now Ethel," soothed Bert, "he'll get used to it—I did."

*

What do you call a virgin on a waterbed?

A cherry float.

*

What do you do when your Kotex catches fire?

Throw it on the floor and tampon it.

*

There are three women on the fast track in a particular company. The president realizes it's time to promote one of them, but they're all so competent he's not sure which to choose. So he devises a little test. One day while they're all at lunch, he places $500 on each of their desks.

#1 returns it to him immediately.

#2 invests in the market and returns $1,500 to him the next morning.

#3 pockets it.

Who gets the promotion? The one with the big tits!

*

What's 10, 9, 8, 7, 6, 5, 4, 3, 2, 1?

Bo Derek getting older.

*

There was this young woman who was really depressed because she was so flat-chested. One day her fairy godmother appeared and offered to grant her most heartfelt wish.

"I want big tits," said the young woman instantly.

"All right, my dear," said the fairy godmother. "From this moment on, every time a man says 'Pardon' to you, they'll get bigger."

The next day the woman is walking down the street, lost in thought, when she bumps into a policeman.

"Pardon me," says the cop politely.

Her tits grow an inch. She's ecstatic. A few days later she goes into a supermarket and comes out with a huge bag of groceries, which she drops when she bumps into a checkout clerk.

"Pardon me," says the clerk, bending over to help her collect her purchases.

Her tits grow another inch. She's beside herself with joy. She goes into a Chinese restaurant and collides with a waiter, who bows and says, "Oh, I beg of you a thousand pardons."

The newspaper headlines the next day proclaim: "CHINESE WAITER KILLED BY TWO TORPEDOES!"

*

Did you hear about the new douche powder made of alum, LSD, and Kentucky Fried Chicken batter?

It's uptight, outasight, and finger-lickin' good.

*

What's the difference between a light bulb and a pregnant woman?

You can unscrew a light bulb.

*

What do fat girls and mopeds have in common?

They're both fun to ride until a friend sees you.

*

Why are women giving up bowling for screwing?

The balls are lighter and you don't have to change your shoes.

*

What's the difference between a job and a wife?

After five years, the job still sucks.

How do you make paper dolls?
    Screw an old bag.

*

What's the white stuff you find in women's panties?
    Clitty litter.

*

Bumper sticker: Support E.R.A.—make him sleep on the wet spot.

*

What do you call a rehabilitation home for ex-prostitutes?
    An all-the-way house.

*

Definition of a wife: "An attachment you screw on the bed to get the housework done."

*

How are an oven and a woman alike?
    You have to get them both hot before you can stick the meat in.

*

Remember what's worse than getting raped by Jack the Ripper? (Getting fingered by Captain Hook.) Well, you know what's worse than *that*?
    Getting eaten out by Jaws.

What's the purpose of a bellybutton?
To put your gum in on the way down.

*

What's the last sound you hear before a pubic hair hits the ground?
(Make a spitting sound.)

*

Why was the stamp commemorating prostitution so unpopular?
You had to pay an extra ten cents to lick it.

*

What's the difference between a hormone and an enzyme?
You can't hear an enzyme.

*

How do you make a hormone?
Put sand in the Vaseline.

*

What's a cunt that talks back?
An answering cervix.

*

What do you give an eighty-year-old woman for her birthday?
Mikey . . . He'll eat anything.

What do you call a woman who uses too much contraceptive cream?

A spermicidal maniac.

*

Once during her summer vacation the Bionic Woman took an overnight train journey. She entered her berth without noticing that the man in the berth above hers was peeping through the curtains. The fellow was quite chagrined to see her remove her wig, false eyelashes, glass eye, padded brassiere, mechanical hand, and bionic leg. When she turned around to pull up the covers she saw the peeping Tom and cried out in alarm, "Oh, my goodness! What do you want?"

"You know damn well what I want," he snarled. "Unscrew it and toss it up here!"

*

A newlywed couple check into a quiet, out-of-the-way lakeside hotel. The clerk and the bellhop tip broad winks at each other, smiling in anticipation of the honeymoon antics to come. But lo and behold, in the middle of the night (their first) who but the groom tromps down the stairs fully laden with fishing gear! This happens again on the second and third nights. The clerk and bellhop can contain their curiosity no longer:

"You're *fishing* in the middle of the night on your honeymoon? Why aren't you up making love to your wife?"

The groom looked bewildered. "Make love to her? Oh no, she's got gonorrhea."

Embarrassed silence. "Oh. What about anal sex?"

"Oh no, she's got diarrhea."
"I see. Well, there's oral sex. . . ."
"Oh no. She's got pyorrhea as well."
"Gonorrhea, diarrhea, *and* pyorrhea! Why, may I ask, did you marry her?"
"Because she's got worms and I just *love* to fish."

*

So the teacher instructs her third-grade class to give a three-syllable word and use it in a sentence. Several pupils raise their hands, including dirty Johnny. Teacher passes him over and chooses Sally.
"Beautiful," Sally says. "My teacher is beautiful!"
"Why, thank you," teacher replies. "Anyone else?" Again, several hands, including Johnny's, are waving. She chooses Mary.
"Wonderful. My teacher is wonderful!" Again the teacher thanks her student, and asks for another answer. Reluctantly, she chooses Johnny.
"Urinate," says Johnny.
"Johnny!!" the teacher replies, shocked.
"Urinate, but if your tits were bigger, you'd be a ten!"

*

A couple were indulging in sexual intercourse and the man noticed that with each movement of his pelvis, his partner's toes would rise. Later that night, while going at it pretty hot and heavy in the shower, her toes remained still. Confused, he asked, "Why is it that when we do it in the bed, your toes go up, but when we do it in the shower, they don't?"

"Silly," she replied, "I take my pantyhose off in the shower!"

*

First Woman: "This is very embarrassing, but every time I sneeze, I have an orgasm."
Second Woman: "You poor dear! Are you taking anything for that?"
First Woman: "Snuff."

Herpes

How does herpes leave the hospital?
On crotches.

*

Seen the new bumpersticker?
Herpes, the love bug.

*

A man was out walking his dog, and a woman stopped to admire the animal. "What's your dog's name?" she asked.

"Herpes," replied the dog's owner.

"How . . . odd," said the woman. "Why Herpes?"

"Because he won't heel."

*

What do you call an Indian with herpes?
Chief Running Sore.

*

What do you get when you fuck a Coke?
Burpies.

*

What's the difference between a midget con artist and a case of herpes?
One's a cunning runt. . . .

A Polish man made the acquaintance of a young woman in a bar, and she accepted his invitation to come back to his apartment. After a few drinks and some soft music the Pole suggested retiring to the bedroom, and the young woman was willing. Soon they were going at it hot and heavy.

Right in the middle of everything the Pole stopped dead, looked at her, and said, "Hey, you don't have herpes, do you?"

"NO!" she said. "Why would you ask that?"

"That's a relief," said the Pole. "The last girl didn't tell me until it was too late."

Leper

Why did the leper fail his driving test?

He left his foot on the gas.

*

What did the leper who was trying to lift something heavy say to the other leper?

"Give me a hand."

*

"Mrs. Morris, can Scotty come out to play?"

"Now, children, you know Scotty has leprosy."

"Well, can we come in and watch him rot?"

*

Did you hear about the leper who robbed a house?

He was doing fine until the dog started barking, and then he went all to pieces.

*

A leper who was so ashamed of his appearance that he hadn't been out of the house in ten years was finally persuaded to take his family out to a restaurant in the neighborhood. While waiting for his order, he noticed a man in the corner pointing and laughing. "What's so funny, buddy?" the leper asked, walking over to him.

"Nothing at all," replied the man, but no sooner had the leper sat down again than he noticed a woman cracking up at another table. "You got a problem, lady?" he asked, but she just kept shaking her head until he sat down again.

When a third person, a pleasant-looking young man, started roaring with laughter, the leper was unable to contain himself. Grabbing the young man by the lapels, he hissed, "Why the hell are all you people laughing at me?"

"Oh, it's not you," assured the young man, wiping the tears from his eyes. "It's the fellow behind you dipping his bread in your back."

*

What's the leper theme song?

"Put Your Head on My Shoulders."

And the runner-up?

"I Wanna Hold Your Hand."

*

What do you call a leper with herpes?

Redundant.

*

What do you call a leper with herpes who also has AIDS?

Trendy.

*

How did the leper castrate himself?

Jerking off.

How come the leper couldn't speak?
The cat got his tongue.

*

Why was the leper kicked off the relay team?
He lost the last leg.

*

How come no one in the leper colony could walk after the war?
Because they were defeated.

*

Did you hear about the leper colony against nuclear proliferation?
They're already disarmed.

*

How come the leper couldn't tie his new, expensive running shoes?
They cost him an arm and a leg.

*

Why did the leper pitcher retire?
He threw his arm out.

*

What's small, green, and falls apart?
A leperchaun.

*

Did you hear about the new social program in the leper colony?

Government handouts.

*

How do you make a skeleton?

Put a leper in a wind tunnel.

And how do you make leper sausage?

Put a sock at the other end.

*

What did the captain say to the leper crew?

All hands on deck.

Homosexual

Know what GAY stands for?
Got AIDS Yet?

*

What do you call a faggot in a wheelchair?
Rolaids.

*

A gay guy came into his doctor's office and said, "Doc, I think I've got VD."

"From whom?" asked the doctor.

"How should I know? You think I've got eyes in the back of my head?"

*

Two gay guys are standing looking out at the river, watching the boats go by. "Say, Larry," says Pete, "what kind of boat is that one, the one with all the cars on it?"

"You silly," answers Larry. "That's a ferry boat."

"Wow," says Pete. "I knew we were popular, but I didn't know we had our own navy!"

*

If there were a fag on your back, would you beat him off?

Hear about the new disease gay musicians are coming down with?

Bandaids.

*

Three gays were discussing what they thought their favorite sport would be. The first decides on football, 'cause of all those gorgeous guys bending over in their tight pants.

"Definitely wrestling," sighs the second guy. "Those skimpy little costumes, and think of the holds."

"Definitely baseball," says the third guy. "Why? Well, I'd be pitching with the bases loaded, the batter would hit a line drive right to me, I'd catch it, and I'd just stand there while the other guys rounded the bases. Meanwhile the crowd would be going crazy, screaming, 'Throw the ball, you cocksucker!' and that's what I like—recognition."

*

Did you hear about the two Irish gays?

Patrick Fitzhenry and Henry Fitzpatrick.

*

Four faggots were sitting in a hot tub when a blob of semen rose to the surface. One said, "All right, who farted?"

In the bathroom on the 21st floor of the Empire State Building a faggot made the mistake of coming on to a musclebound Marine, who proceeded to throw him out the window. When the Marine came out onto the street he walked right past the fag lying bleeding in the gutter. Raising himself painfully on one elbow, the fag said, "Yoo-hoo—I'm not angry!"

*

What do fags drink?
Kool-AIDS.

*

Hear about the gay guy who went to the chair and wanted to blow the fuse?

*

How about the new breakfast cereal called Queerios?
You add milk and they eat themselves.

*

How do lesbians kiss?
With their lips.

*

These two gays wake up one morning and one of them says to the other, "This is terrible. One of us is simply going to have to get a job." The other one says, "You're right. I'll go." So he gets out of bed, takes a shower, and puts on a jacket and tie, but when he walks into the kitchen he sees his lover jerking off into a plastic bag.

"What are you doing *that* for?" he asks.

"Well," says the first gay, "I didn't think you'd be coming home for lunch so I thought I'd pack you one."

*

What do you call a fag with diarrhea?

A juicyfruit.

*

What do gay termites eat?

Woody Woodpeckers.

*

Why did Frosty the Snowman pull down his pants?

He heard the snowblower coming.

*

A big tough guy whose wife has just left him is drowning his sorrow at the bar when a flamboyant faggot swishes up to him, simpers, and says, "Hey, wanna play some bar football?"

"Fuck off, faggot."

"C'mon, big boy," insists the fag. "Try bar football—you'll like it."

Sunk in misery and self-pity, the guy finally gives in. "Fuck, what is it, anyway?"

"You down a pint of beer and that's a touchdown," explains the fag excitedly, "then drop your pants and fart for the extra point."

Feeling he has nothing to lose, the guy says, "Shit, okay."

"I'll go first," shrieks the gay, quickly downing his beer. "Touchdown, six points," he yells, then just as quickly drops trou and emits a high, squeaky fart. "Seven to zip, your turn!"

The tough guy chugs his beer, then unenthusiastically pulls down his pants. In a flash the fag leaps behind him and sticks a finger up his ass, squealing, "Block that kick! Block that kick!"

*

What do you call a gay dentist?

A tooth fairy.

*

How do you get rid of crabs?

Find a faggot who likes seafood.

And if that doesn't work?

Shave off half your pubic hair. Get a match and a hammer. Set the rest of your pubic hair on fire, and when the crabs run out, beat them to death with the hammer.

*

Did you hear about the queer nail?

It lay in the road and blew a tire.

*

A gay guy walks into a bar in the Deep South with a huge German shepherd. When he walks up to the bar and asks for a scotch and water, the bartender looks him over and replies, "We don't serve your kind in here."

"Say," says the gay, "I'm pretty thirsty, and if I don't get a drink soon I'll sic my dog Killer on you."

"Listen, faggot," snarls the bartender. "Get out of here or I'll throw you out. And I ain't scared of your dog!"

"You've forced my hand," says the gay, reaching down to unsnap the leash. "Go, Killer, get him!" So Killer jumps up on the counter and scratches the bartender's eyes out.

*

What's in the air in San Francisco that keeps women from getting pregnant?

Men's legs.

*

What's a fellatio teacher?

A headmaster.

*

Why don't faggots lean on baseball bats with their rear ends?

They're afraid it might get serious.

*

What's worse than a six-foot Negro with a switchblade?

A queer with a chipped tooth.

Three gays were sitting around and the conversation turned to their innermost fantasies.

"I'd like to be a flower and be thmelled by everyone," lisped the first.

"Fabulous," ejaculated the second, adding, "I'd like to be an ice cream cone and have everyone take a slurp."

"How naive," squealed the third. "I'd like to be an ambulance: My rear doors would be opened wide, the patient would be shoved in, and I'd shriek, "OOOH-AAAH-OOOH-AAAH-OOOH-AAAH....'"

*

A truckdriver is rolling down the interstate when he sees two fags hitchiking, and, being a nice guy, he stops to pick them up. A couple of miles down the road, the first fag asks politely, "May I fart?"

"Sure," says the truckdriver heartily. "Blow your ass out." So the fag lets loose one HUGE fart, so juicy that all the windows steam up. A few miles later, the second fag inquires of the truckdriver whether he can cut one also.

"Go right ahead," says the trucker. "My wife puts plenty of holes in these seats." So the second fag lets loose one even juicier than the first fag's.

A little later, when the windows have cleared, the truckdriver says, "Would you guys mind if I farted?" Reassured to the contrary, he farts, but it's so tiny it can hardly even be heard.

Looking at each other knowingly, the fags say in unison, "We know who's a virgin!"

*

What did the gay paramedic give his lover?
First AIDS.

*

What do you call a black fag in a wheelchair?
Cool AIDS.

*

What do you get if you listen to too many obscene phone calls?
Hearing AIDS.

*

What do you call a gay bar with no stools?
A fruit stand.

*

Did you hear that Ben Hur had a sex change operation?
Now he's Ben Gay.

*

Two gays are walking down the street one day when they pass a particularly handsome man.

"See that guy who just walked by," said one of the gay men. "He's a good fuck."

"No shit?" exclaimed his friend.

"Well, hardly any."

*

What do you call a couple of gay lawyers?
Legal AIDS.

Four men in a bar are having an argument over whose cock is bigger. After a while the bartender tires of these men yelling and not drinking, so he says, "Okay, you guys, unzip and whip 'em out onto the bar." As they do so, a little fag walks in. "Oh, my!" he exclaims.

"Whadda you want?" the bartender asks the fag.

"Well, I was going to have a Black Russian, but now I think I'll have the buffet."

*

Did you hear about the gay guy who flew to London?

He was heartbroken when he found out Big Ben was a clock!

*

Did you hear about the new gay bar?

It's called Boys-r-us.

"Mommy, Mommy"

"Mommy, Mommy, can I lick the bowl?"
"Shut up and flush the toilet."

*

"Mommy, Mommy, can I buy a new dress?"
"You know it won't fit over your iron lung."

*

"Mommy, Mommy, this doesn't taste like tomato juice."
"Shut up and drink it before it clots."

*

"Mommy, Mommy, why do I keep going in circles?"
"Shut up or I'll nail your other foot to the floor."

*

"Mommy, Mommy, do we have to visit Grandma again?"
"Shut up and keep digging."

*

"Mommy, Mommy, I don't want hamburger for dinner."
"Shut up or I'll stick your other arm in the meat grinder."

"Mommy, Mommy, do we have to have spaghetti again tonight?"

"Shut up or I'll pull the veins out of your other leg."

*

"Mommy, Mommy, why can't I play with the other kids?"

"Shut up and deal."

*

"Mommy, Mommy, why is everyone running away?"

"Shut up and reload."

Religion

Sister Mary Ignatius was quite flattered to be invited by the Bishop to play golf one Saturday afternoon. When the Bishop missed a putt on the 16th hole, however, she was shocked to hear him say, "Fuckin' shit, I missed!"

"I'm deeply ashamed of you," said a white-faced Sister Mary Ignatius.

The Bishop shot her a dirty look and went on toward the 17th hole. Not long afterward he exclaimed, "Fuckin' shit, I missed!"

"I'm warning you, Bishop," said the nun piously. "God will strike you down if you don't stop using that kind of language."

The Bishop also missed the crucial putt on the 18th hole, and uttered the same curses at full volume. Suddenly there was a deafening clap of thunder, a blinding flash of lightning, and the nun disappeared.

A few seconds later boomed a voice from the heavens, "FUCKIN' SHIT, I MISSED!"

*

A nun walked into the corner liquor store and asked the proprietor for a fifth of whisky.

"Sister, now how would it look for a respectable fellow like me to sell alcohol to a nun?" was the reply.

The woman leaned over the counter and whispered conspiratorially, "It's really for the Mother Superior's constipation."

The store owner thought it over and decided to sell it to her since it was for medicinal purposes, but only on condition that she hide it in a paper bag and not tell anyone.

An hour later the store owner closed up and walked outside, only to immediately come across the nun on a park bench, roaring drunk.

"Sister," he said angrily, "you know I only sold you that whisky because it was to ease Mother Superior's constipation."

"It ish," slurred the nun. "When she sees me, she'll shit."

*

What's another reason God created the orgasm?

Because He couldn't wait for the second coming.

*

Two leprechauns arrived at the convent door and asked to speak with the Mother Superior. Led into her office, the first one asked respectfully, "Excuse me, your holiness, but are there any leprechaun nuns at this convent?"

Receiving a reply in the negative, he asked whether any leprechaun nuns were to be found in the neighboring parish. Again the reply was no.

The tiny man scratched his head and posed a final question. "Beggin' your pardon, Mother Superior, but would you know of *any* leprechaun nuns at all, anywhere?" The nun shook her head.

At which the second leprechaun shook the first by the shoulders, and shouted, "You see! You see! I told you you fucked a penguin!"

What's the difference between Jesus Christ and an oil painting?

You only need one nail to hang up a painting.

*

A priest and a rabbi decided to pool their money and buy a car, since neither could afford one on his own. On the day of the purchase, they made an agreement at the Toyota dealership that the vehicle would not be more of one religion than of the other.

The priest was a very devout fellow, however, and the very first night, unaware of the rabbi spying on him through the keyhole, he snuck into the garage and sprinkled a little holy water on the hood.

The next night, very cautiously, the rabbi tiptoed into the garage. Hacksaw in hand, he proceeded to take four inches off the tailpipe....

*

What do you get when you mix holy water with castor oil?

A religious movement.

*

A man is driving along a country road when his car breaks down. He has it towed to the nearest repair shop, which happens to be next door to a convent. Told that the car will take an hour to fix, he pays a visit to the convent and ends up spending the hour in bed with young Sister Angela. As they finish their lovemaking they hear someone coming, so the man sprints off naked over the convent wall while Sister Angela ditches his clothes in the laundry room.

That night all the nuns are called together to a special meeting, and a chorus of gasps follow the Mother Superior's announcement that a man's clothing had been found inside the convent.

"We found a man's shirt!" thunders the head nun. All the nuns gasp, but a single giggle escapes from Sister Angela.

"And we found a man's trousers!" continues Mother Superior. All the nuns gasp; Sister Angela giggles.

"And we found a man's underwear!" All the nuns gasp; Sister Angela giggles.

"And we found a condom!" Again a chorus of gasps, and a single giggle from the back of the room.

"*And*," goes on the Mother Superior, "we found a hole in the condom!"

And all the nuns giggle as Sister Angela gasps.

*

What happened to the Pope when he went to Mount Olive?

Popeye almost killed him.

*

A priest and a rabbi were sitting next to each other on an airplane when the captain announced a little engine trouble . . . and a little rough weather . . . and finally suggested that anyone on board who is religiously inclined say their last prayers. The priest fell to his knees in the aisle, and as he crossed himself he noticed the rabbi doing the same thing. So when the plane leveled off and things began to look more hopeful, he turned to the rabbi and said smugly, "So, when you truly feared death, you turned to Almighty Jesus for solace!"

"Not at all." The rabbi smiled, repeating his gestures. "The usual check: spectacles, testicles, money, and cigars!"

*

An unwed pregnant girl went to the doctor for an abortion, but found to her dismay that things were too far along. "Don't worry," said the kind-hearted doctor, "when your time comes, go into the hospital and have the baby. There's sure to be someone in for a gallbladder operation, and we'll give her the baby and tell her it wasn't her gallbladder after all."

She followed his plan, but when the baby was born the only gallbladder case in the hospital was a middle-aged priest. What the hell, thought the doctor, I'll give it a try. So he presented the baby to the priest, who was overjoyed. "This is an act of God," he exclaimed happily and took the infant home. They lived a contented life together for twenty years, until the priest found himself on his deathbed.

He called the boy in and said, "My son, I must tell you something. I'm not really your father—I'm your mother. The Bishop is your father."

*

What do they make from frozen holy water?

Popesicles.

Jesus, Moses, and an old man are playing golf. Moses tees up and hits his ball into the water trap. Nonplussed, he goes over to the lake, parts the water with his club, and hits his ball onto the green.

Jesus tees up next, and also manages to land in the water trap. So he walks down to the lake, across the water, and hits his ball out onto the green.

Last to tee up is the old man, whose ball heads straight for the water. As the ball hits the surface a fish jumps up and swallows it but is immediately grabbed by an eagle, which deposits the fish on the green. The ball shoots out of the fish's mouth and rolls into the cup.

Jesus turns around and says, "Nice shot, Dad, but would you quit fucking around and play golf?"

*

Three nuns are waiting for an audience with Mother Theresa. The first nun goes in and says, "Forgive me, Mother, but I've seen a man's privates."

"Go wash your eyes in holy water," says Mother Theresa.

The second nun confesses to Mother Theresa that she has touched a man's privates. "My child," says the elderly nun, "go wash your hands in holy water."

The two nuns are busy with their penance when the third nun comes over and says, "Watch out, girls—I gotta gargle."

There was bad flooding in New Orleans one spring, and the water was up to the porch of the parish priest's house when a jeep drove by to pick him up. "Don't save me, save someone more needy," said the devout old man.

Eight hours later the water was up past the second story and the priest was on the roof when the rescue boat came by. "Go save someone else," he said.

After another eight hours the water was up to the man's chin, and a helicopter came by with a rope. "No, no," he said, "save someone else first," and he resumed his prayers. About ten minutes later he drowned, of course, and went to heaven. It wasn't until two weeks later that he got to meet God.

"God," he said, "what happened? I've been a believer all my life and I just knew that You would save me."

God answered, "Well, you damn fool, first I sent a jeep, then a boat, and then a helicopter!"

*

A black greets a fellow black on the street: "Hey, mothafuckah!"

"Good morning, Reverend."

*

Every Sunday down in Macon, Georgia, this Southern Baptist, a good ol' boy, picks up the minister to take him to church. One morning the fellow notices a bunch of black guys hanging out by the side of the road. He's dying to run them over, but he doesn't quite dare, since the minister's in the car right next to him. So he takes out his handkerchief and, pretending to sneeze, swerves wildly over the sidewalk.

"Did I hit any? Did I hit any?" he asks, trying to instill a note of genuine panic into his voice.

"Naw," drawled the minister, "but I got two of the muthas with the door."

*

Why don't black women make good nuns?

They can't say "superior" after "mother."

*

An insurance salesman dies and goes to heaven, only to find a long, long line waiting at the pearly gates. He waits and waits for hours, talking to the others in line: cops, clerks, and people from all professions. As they are talking, they see a man dressed in white, carrying a medical bag, approach the head of the line. He says a couple of words to St. Peter and is immediately ushered into heaven. The salesman is irate. He wasn't pushed around in life, and he doesn't want to get pushed around now. He makes his way to the head of the line and lets St. Peter have it. "I've been waiting here for hours, and some damn doctor pushes his way into heaven. What gives?" St. Peter replies, "Don't get so upset. That was just God playing doctor."

*

A nervous young priest, about to deliver his first sermon, asks an older priest how he might calm down a bit. He advises the young priest to fill the water pitcher with martinis. Well, the new priest preaches up a storm, and afterwards he asks the older priest what he thought.

"You did very well, but I have just a few criticisms:

—There are ten commandments, not twelve.

—There are twelve apostles, not ten.

—David slew Goliath; he did not 'kick the shit out of Goliath.'

—Next week there is a taffy pull at St. Peter's, not a Peter pull at St. Taffy's.

—The holy cross is not to be referred to as 'the Big T.'

—Please do not refer to Our Savior Jesus Christ and the apostles as 'J.C. and the boys.'

—And restrain yourself from calling the Father, the Son, and the Holy Ghost 'Big Daddy, Junior, and the Spook.'

—And lastly, kindly do not call the Blessed Virgin Mary 'Mary with the cherry.'"

Cruelty to Animals

Mr. Johnson went out on his annual hunting expedition and actually succeeded in bagging a pheasant. He proudly brought it home and did his best to clean it, and that night the family sat down to a pheasant dinner. After a few mouthfuls his wife jumped up and ran for the bathroom. She came back a few minutes later and said, "Honey, there were little black things in my shit. What do you think it could be?"

"Uh-oh," said Mr. Johnson, "I guess I didn't clean the pheasant out too well. Just keep an eye out for the birdshot while you're eating."

About five minutes later his daughter dashed for the bathroom. She came out crying, "Daddy, Daddy, there's black things floating in my pee!"

"Pellets again—I'm really sorry. Don't worry, they won't hurt you," he reassured her.

Soon enough his son strolled off, coming back to the table ten minutes later. "What's wrong with you, Billy?" asked Mr. Johnson.

"I was jerking off and I shot the dog."

*

You know what elephants use for tampons, right?

Sheep.

But do you know why elephants have trunks?

Because sheep don't have strings.

*

Why don't chickens wear underwear?

Because their peckers are on their faces.

What kind of bees give the most milk?
Boo bees.

*

"Daddy, what are those two dogs doing?"
"Uhh . . . one's sick and the other one's pushing him to the hospital."

*

One day Father O'Malley was walking through the park when he came upon an enchanting scene. A beautiful little girl with long blond hair, deep blue eyes, and a dainty white lace dress was playing under a tree with her adorable little dog.

What a lovely picuture, thought Father O'Malley to himself. Walking over, he asked, "Child, what is your name?"

"Blossom," she replied.

"What a fitting name," exclaimed Father O'Malley. "And how did your parents come to choose such a pretty name?"

"Well, one day when I was still in my mommie's tummy she was lying under this very tree when a blossom fell and landed on her stomach. She thought it was a message from God and decided that if I were a girl, my name would be Blossom," explained the little girl sweetly.

How charming, thought the priest. He started to walk away, then turned back. "And the name of your little dog?" he inquired.

"Porky," was the child's reply.

Again he asked her how the unusual name had been chosen.

"Because he likes to fuck pigs."

What's the best way to catch a fish?
Have someone throw it to you.

*

Did you hear about the Purdue student who was majoring in animal husbandry?
They caught him at it.

*

A bear and a rabbit are taking a crap in the woods. The bear looks over at the rabbit and asks, "Say, does shit ever stick to your fur?"

"No."

So the bear wiped his ass with the rabbit.

*

An Alabama deputy sheriff went fishing on his day off. As he sat on the riverbank, a kid came walking by. Spying a frog, the kid grabbed it, took out his pocket knife, and said, "Frog, I's gon' cut yo' legs off!" Then he said, "Frog, after I gets done cuttin' yo legs off, I's gon' stick this here Popsicle stick up yo' rear end! And then, Frog . . ."

This was too much for the deputy. He stood up, grabbed the kid, and said, "Looka heah, boy, whatever you do to that frog, I'm gonna do to you!"

The kid said, "Frog, dis here's yo' lucky day, 'cause I's gon' kiss yo' ass."

*

How do you make a bull sweat?
Give him a tight jersey.

Female centipede (crossing her legs): "For the 100th time, no!"

*

What did Tarzan say when the elephants came over the hill?

"The elephants are coming! The elephants are coming!"

What did Tarzan say when the elephants came over the hill with glasses on?

Nothing. He didn't recognize them.

*

How do you eat a frog?

Put one leg over each ear.

*

Have you heard of the new Oriental cookbook?

It's called *101 Ways to Wok Your Dog*.

*

What did the goldfish say to the Polack?

"We don't swim in your john, so please don't pee in our pool."

*

A streetcorner violinist heard a grunt and turned to see two dogs screwing. The one on top said to him, "Well, don't just stand there—play *Bolero*."

Why did the monkey fall out of the tree?
It was dead.

*

What's the big drag about fucking a cow?
You have to climb down from the stump and walk around front every time you want to kiss her.

*

What do you call an experimental monkey in a Cuisinart?
Rhesus Pieces.

*

A young woman had recently moved into a condominium in a very elite part of town, when she decided that what she needed to go with her posh new surroundings was a new pet. Not just any ordinary pet, but an exotic one that would fit in with her new abode. The woman went into a nearby pet store and asked the owner what he had in the way of exotic pets.

"Well," said the pet store owner, "I'm afraid all that I have left to offer you is a bullfrog that sells for five hundred dollars."

"Five hundred dollars!" exclaimed the woman.

"For a bullfrog? What could possibly make a bullfrog worth five hundred dollars?" she asked.

"Well," said the store owner sheepishly, "this bullfrog is trained in the art of cunnilingus."

"Now *that* sounds intriguing," said the woman. After a moment or two of thought, she handed over the five hundred dollars and ran home, anxious to see her new pet perform.

As soon as she got home, she quickly undressed, lay on the bed, legs spread, and placed the frog between her thighs. The frog sat motionless, refusing to budge.

"Brrrrp," croaked the bullfrog, but it remained still. The woman nudged the frog a few times, but the frog remained motionless, letting out an occasional "Brrrrp," but nothing more.

Furious, the woman threw on her bathrobe, frog in hand, and stormed out of her condo and down the street to the pet store.

"I want my money back!" she yelled, slamming the poor bullfrog down on the countertop.

"I beg your pardon?" asked the store owner.

"You told me this damn bullfrog was trained in the art of cunnilingus. Well, I took him home and he does nothing but croak."

"Are you quite sure?" asked the owner.

Incensed at this point, the woman threw off her bathrobe, jumped up on the counter, put the frog between her legs as before, and waited.

"Brrrrp," croaked the frog, motionless.

"See!" cried the woman. "I told you."

At which point the store owner stuck his head between the woman's legs and whispered in the frog's ear, "All right, you little son of a bitch, I'm going to show you just one more time."

Two men are standing around talking while nearby a large hound lay licking his balls. One man says to the other, "Gee, I wish I could do that." The other man replies, "I think you should get to know him first."

*

If an elephant's front legs were going 60 MPH, what would its back legs be doing?

Hauling ass, baby, hauling ass.

*

What do you call a cow with no legs?

Ground beef.

Miscellaneous

What's the difference between an oral and a rectal thermometer?
The taste.

*

What's the definition of "thorny"?
A thailor at thea.

*

Why did the undertaker serve cola at the funeral?
Coke adds life.

*

What's the difference between like and love?
A spit and a swallow.

*

What gets wetter as it dries?
Toilet paper.

*

An eight-year-old boy dressed up as a pirate went trick-or-treating on Halloween. He knocked on a door, and an old lady came out and said, "Oh, a pirate! How cute! And where are your buccaneers?"

"They're right under my buck'n hat, lady."

Why is dealing with the IRS like wearing a rubber?

You get the feeling of safety and security while being screwed with no sensitivity at all.

*

A new drink's been invented—

It's one part vodka and one part prune juice, and it's called a pile driver.

*

What's the difference between a fashion model and a prostitute?

Prostitutes don't drive Ferraris.

*

"Patty," scolded Mrs. Wilson, "you knew very well the train would run over little Terence when you put him on the tracks."

"I gave him a timetable, didn't I?"

*

What does a man do standing up, a woman do sitting down, and a dog do with one leg raised?

Shake hands.

*

What's black and yellow and full of little Crispy Critters?

A burnt schoolbus.

A plane is flying in a storm and lightning hits the main engine. It becomes evident that the plane's going down, and a few minutes later it crashes in the ocean. The captain's voice comes over the intercom: "All passengers who can swim, please get to the left side of the aisle and prepare to abandon the aircraft. All passengers who can't swim, please keep to the right side of the plane. Now, passengers on the left, jump out and swim for that little island! Passengers on the right, thank you for flying with us."

*

Did you hear about the new designer condoms?
They're called "Sergio Prevente."

*

Why is San Francisco like granola?
Because once you get past the fruits and the nuts, all you have left is the flakes.

*

"Michael, stop twisting your sister's head."
"Michael, I SAID to stop that!"
"I'm going to belt you one if you don't stop twisting Lisa's head!"
"Okay, Michael, give it back to her."

*

What's worse than lipstick on your collar?
Leg makeup on your ears.

What's 69 twice?
Dinner for four.

*

What did Mr. Spock find in the toilet?
The Captain's log.

*

Why did Captain Kirk pee on the ceiling?
To go where no man has ever gone before.

*

What do toilet paper and the starship *Enterprise* have in common?
They both circle Uranus looking for Klingons.

*

What's blue and creamy?
Smurf cum.

*

For months the loving newlywed had asked his bride to give him oral sex, but to no avail. His sweet entreaties never worked, for the blushing bride was simply too innocent and inexperienced to even *think* of such a thing, let alone attempt it. But a year of gentle persistence finally paid off, and one night his darling nervously but lovingly performed the act. When it was over, she looked deeply into his eyes and asked, "How was I, sweetheart?"

He looked back at her and said, "How should I know—I'm no cocksucker!"

Why can't witches have babies?
Their husbands have Halloweenies.

*

Why can't fortune tellers have babies?
Their husbands have crystal balls.

*

What's yellow and green and eats nuts?
Gonorrhea.

*

What happens when you cross a prostitute with a computer?
You get a fucking know-it-all.

*

What do the Moral Majority and the gay community have in common?
They both suck.

*

Know where you can find sympathy?
In the dictionary, somewhere between "shit" and "syphilis."

*

Helen's husband had a terrible habit of letting go with an absolutely gigantic fart every time he woke up in the morning. His wife's warnings that one day he was going to fart his guts right out had no effect on Sam.

One Thanksgiving morning Helen was up early preparing the turkey dinner when the perfect way to stop Sam's disgusting habit came into her head. She took the giblets from the turkey, snuck into the bedroom, and very carefully dropped them down the back of Sam's shorts.

Sam woke up and cut a huge fart, but when he rolled over onto his back he felt something strange. Fearing the worst, he ran into the bathroom, and Helen was gratified to hear a terrifying shriek through the closed door.

When she came up the stairs to check on him, Sam was white as a ghost and dripping with sweat. Holding up two fingers, he said, "My God, Helen, you were right! I farted my guts right out, but by the grace of God and these two fingers I got 'em all back in!"

*

What's green and yellow, has cookie crumbs all over it, lies on the side of the road, and stinks?

A dead Girl Scout.

*

Five people—the pilot, the Pope, the president of the United States, a famous black leader, and a Boy Scout—were traveling in a light plane. When one of the plane's engines sputtered and caught fire, the pilot, realizing that the plane was going down, made an announcement to his alarmed passengers.

"Gentlemen," he said, "we aren't going to make it. Not only that, but we've only got *four* parachutes for the *five* of us. I hate to be selfish about this, but the early bird gets the worm. Adios!"

So saying, he grabbed one of the four parachutes and leaped from the plane.

The president then turned to his fellow passengers. "My survival is crucial to the well-being of the free world," he intoned. "I must think of the country . . . and save myself."

And *he* reached into the pile of chutes, took one, and jumped.

Then the black leader seized the moment.

"I am the world's smartest black man," he shouted. "Millions of black people all over the world look to me for leadership. I must think of the future!"

And he reached into the pile and threw himself out the door.

The Pope, a kindly man, turned to the Boy Scout.

"I've lived a long life," he said to the young Scout. "The time has come for me to meet Our Lord. Son, I want you to take that last parachute and save yourself."

The Boy Scout grinned and clapped the Pope on his shoulder.

"It's not your time yet, Pope," he said. "The world's smartest black man just jumped out of here carrying my knapsack!"

*

Two old guys wonder if there's baseball in heaven and promise each other that the first to get there will somehow let the other know. A week later one of them dies. A week after that he contacts his friend on earth and says, "Joe, I've got some good news and some bad news. The good news is that there *is* a baseball team in heaven. The bad news is that you're pitching on Friday."

What's the difference between a fox and a pig?
About 8 or 9 drinks.

*

A young up-and-coming executive was informed that he would be forced to take a 30 percent cut in pay. Later on that evening he was discussing with his wife ways in which they could trim some fat out of their budget.

"Honey," he said, "if you could learn to prepare a few meals, we could fire the cook."

"Well, dear," she replied, "if you could learn to fuck, we could get rid of the gardener."

*

A cannibal went to the witch doctor, complaining of stomach pains. The witch doctor examined him and said, "It must have been something you ate. Tell me about it."

The cannibal replied, "I ate a missionary the other day."

"That shouldn't have done it. Can you remember any details about him?"

"Well, he was a tall man, he was wearing a brown robe, he was walking down the trail, and I caught him and boiled him and ate him."

"That's the trouble, you dummy, you boiled him and he was a friar."

*

What has orange hair, big feet, and comes out of a test tube?
Bozo the Clone.

How do you spot a levelheaded Kentuckian?

He's got tobacco juice running out of *both* corners of his mouth.

*

There is this guy who really takes care of his body. He lifts weights and jogs five miles every day. One morning he looks into the mirror and admires his body. He notices that he is really suntanned all over except on his penis, and decides to do something about it.

He goes to the beach, completely undresses and buries himself in the sand except for his penis, which he leaves sticking out.

Two little old ladies are strolling along the beach, and one looks down and says, "There really is no justice in this world!" The other old lady says, "What do you mean?"

The first old lady says, "look at that!

"When I was 10 years old, I was afraid of it.

"When I was 20 years old, I was curious about it.

"When I was 30 years old, I enjoyed it.

"When I was 40 years old, I asked for it.

"When I was 50 years old, I paid for it.

"When I was 60 years old, I prayed for it.

"When I was 70 years old, I forgot about it.

"And now that I'm 80, the damn things are growing wild."

*

What's the first thing Eskimo mothers teach their children?

Don't eat yellow snow.

What did June Cleaver say when she reached menopause?

"Ward, I'm worried about the Beaver."

*

How many JAPs does it take to screw in a light bulb?

Five: four to bitch about it and one to get her boyfriend to do it.

*

There was once a salesman who had an outstanding record for selling toothbrushes. His boss, wondering at this unlikely success, sent a man out to follow the salesman on rounds to see what pitch he gave that brought such good results. It was soon found that this particular salesman went to the corner of a busy street and opened up his briefcase, and on one side was the assortment of toothbrushes, and on the other side a bag of potato chips and a small bowl of brownish stuff. He would grab a likely customer and give them the following pitch.

"Good morning, ma'am, this is a commercial promotion for———brand of chip dip. Would you care to give it a try?" At that point the person would try it, then spit it out and scream in utter disgust. "This tastes like shit!" The salesman would smile and say, "It is. You want to buy a toothbrush?"

*

A urologist claimed that he could find any disease just by testing a person's urine. One man, who had tennis elbow, decided to fool the doctor. He made an appointment, received his specimen bottle, and was told to come back the next day. That night he urinated in the bottle, then his wife did, followed by his daughter, and then the family dog. Then he beat off in it. He returned the next day with his sample and gave it to the doctor for testing. Four hours went by before the doctor came out. He was just sweating bullets. "You know," he said, "it took me a long time, but I think I've finally got it. Your wife has V.D., your daughter is pregnant, your dog has mange, and if you'd quit beating off, you wouldn't have tennis elbow."

*

Did you hear about the Texan who was so big that when he died, there wasn't a coffin large enough to hold him?

They gave him an enema and buried him in a shoebox.

Too Tasteless to Be Included in This Book

Why can't you go to the bathroom at a Beatles concert?
There's no John.

*

What's grosser than gross?
Fucking a pregnant lady and the fetus gives you head.

*

What's grosser than gross?
Biting into a hot dog and finding veins in it.

*

What's grosser than gross?
When you open the refrigerator door and the rump roast farts in your face.

*

What's grosser than gross?
Finding a pubic hair in your Bloody Mary.

Why were the midget and the circus fat lady so deliriously happy when they were married?

She let him try a new wrinkle every night.

*

Did you hear about the man who ate his son?

He didn't know his wife was pregnant.

*

What do you do with a dead black?

Cut off his lips and use them for suitcase handles.

*

A very horny young man goes to the busiest whorehouse in town, goes up to the front desk, and orders a blonde with big tits. Sitting down on the sofa, he sees a bowl of tomatoes on the coffee table, and being pretty hungry, he reaches over and bites into one. Just then his blonde walks in, but at the sight of him she shrieks and runs back up the stairs.

A bit disconcerted by this performance, the man cancels his order and asks for a redhead with even bigger tits. He's just bitten into a second tomato when a luscious redhead materializes, only to run out of the room with a horror-stricken look on her face.

Thoroughly disgruntled by now, he asks for a brunette, but she too takes one look at him chewing away and runs up the stairs screaming. Going over to the front desk, the young man pounds on the counter and says, "What the hell is goin' on around here? I wanna get laid!"

"You eating the tomatoes over there on that table?" asks the proprietor.

"Yeah, so?"

"Sorry to say, buddy, but those are last week's abortions."

*

What's grosser than gross?

When your girlfriend does a split and your best friend's class ring falls out.

*

What's grosser than gross?

Feeling your grandpa get a hard-on while you're sitting on his lap.

*

A sailor on shore leave lost all but five dollars in a poker game. As he was very horny after several months at sea, he went to the local whorehouse and asked the madam if she had anything available for five bucks. "Well," said the madam after giving it a little thought, "we can give you Beulah. She's a little old, but for five dollars..."

"That's great," said the sailor, handing over his money.

The madam directed him to the last room down the hallway. Inside, he found the oldest, dirtiest, ugliest woman he'd ever seen. But as horny and broke as he was, he figured he'd go for it, first turning off the light so he wouldn't have to look at her.

As soon as he had crawled into bed the crone rasped, "Put it in."

After a few moments, he said, "I can't. It's too dry and scratchy."

"Wait a minute," she said, and she sat up on the side of the bed, fiddling around with her crotch. The sailor couldn't make out what she was doing, but in a few moments she was back in bed. "Now try."

He slipped in with no trouble. In fact, it was as warm and moist as a young woman's. "Hey, this is great!" he exclaimed. "What'd you do, use some kind of special cream or something?"

"Nope," cackled the old woman, "I just picked the scabs off and let the pus run."

Would you like to see your favorite tasteless joke(s) in print? If so, send them to:

Blanche Knott
℅ Ballantine Books
201 East 50th Street
New York, New York 10022

Remember, no compensation or credit can be given, and only those "tasteless" enough will be included!